In Enzo Silon Surin's stellar debut, we find a child cornered on corners, elegy distilled from eulogy, unnerving music after a certain numbness, fury after pain. Everywhere there is the evidence of a body done wrong: poverty mounts on violence, shaping the hand into a fist ready to strike. Yet this book is also profoundly lyrical, sensitive, and altogether loving. Surin's eloquence deserves recognition: these poems are exquisitely crafted. Moreover, *When My Body Was A Clinched Fist* is a deeply important contribution to our national conversation about gun violence.

—CATE MARVIN, author of *Oracle*

In this full-length debut, Enzo Silon Surin traverses the turns of coming of age in the New York of the 1990s. In these sonically-packed stanzas, Surin draws scenes where hip hop and Haiti flow through the borough of Queens. He elegizes a friend named Frankie, and interrogates how masculinity is so often flexed like the knuckles of an ever-ready fist, even when vulnerability pulses underneath.

—TARA BETTS, author of *Break the Habit*

When My Body Was A Clinched Fist emerges as a significant marker in the reimagining of African American culture. Enzo Silon Surin's poetry brings an honest lyricism to the body of work by people of African descent that began in the eighteenth century in a country that struggles to realize its ideals. His delicate unveiling of hurt and courage are the American story in miniature. A young boy from Haiti leaves the dangers of home to confront the unknown dangers of a new home. Surin is the poet as warrior priest, his work the prophet's homily redefining what it means to become and be an American.

—Afaa M. Weaver,
author of *Spirit Boxing*

When My Body Was A Clinched Fist is born out of ultimate pain. Enzo Silon Surin weaves his words, like he weaves through trauma, with vulnerability, grace, and radical resilience. His writing is clearly an intrapsychic reckoning, with wounds and scars deeper than anyone ever wants to ever fathom, and too, a love song to finding home again within one's mind, body, and brain. The reader is gifted with this journey, which is a redemptive one at its core.

—Jennifer R. Wolkin, PhD, Licensed Psychologist & Clinical Neuropsychologist

When My Body Was A Clinched Fist

www.blacklawrence.com
Executive Editor: Diane Goettel

Cover Art: "When I Rule the World" by Carlos Rancaño
Book and Cover Design: Zoe Norvell

Copyright © 2020 Enzo Silon Surin | ISBN: 978-1-62557-147-2

All rights reserved. Except for brief quotations in critical articles or reviews, no part of this bookmay be reproduced in any manner without prior written permission from the publisher: editors@blacklawrencepress.com

Published 2020 by Black Lawrence Press.

Claudia Rankine, excerpt from ["My brothers are notorious..."] from Citizen: An American Lyric. Copyright © 2014 by Claudia Rankine. Reprinted with the permission of The Permissions Company, LLC on behalf of Graywolf Press, www.graywolfpress.org.

Excerpt from "Down Here" from *Bright Dead Things* by Ada Limón. Copyright © 2015 by Ada Limón. Published by Milkweed Editions and reprinted with permission.

Excerpt(s) from THE BODY KEEPS THE SCORE: BRAIN, MIND, AND BODY IN THE HEALING OF TRAUMA by Bessel van der Kolk, copyright © 2014 by Bessel van der Kolk. Used by permission of Viking Books, an imprint of Penguin Publishing Group, a division of Penguin Random House LLC. All rights reserved

Excerpt from "The Whole Self" from *Words Under the Words: Selected Poems* by Naomi Shihab Nye, copyright © 1995. Reprinted with the permission of Far Corner Books.

Excerpt from "Travel Elegy" from VIEW WITH A GRAIN OF SAND: Selected poems by Wislawa Szymborksa, translated from the Polish by Stanislaw Baranczak and Clare Cavanagh. Copyright © 1995 by Houghton Mifflin Harcourt Publishing Company. Copyright © Czytelnik, Warszawa. Reprinted by permission of Houghton Mifflin Harcourt Publishing Company. All rights reserved.

Gary Jackson, excerpt from "Cornell" from Missing You Metropolis. Copyright © 2010 by Gary Jackson. Reprinted with the permission of The Permissions Company, LLC on behalf of Graywolf Press, Minneapolis, Minnesota, www.graywolfpress.org.

"House Arrest" was originally published in *Resisting the Anomie* copyright © 1995 by Kwame Dawes. Reprinted by permission of Goose Lane Editions.

Lawrence Raab, "Last Restoration" from *Mistaking Each Other for Ghosts*. Copyright © 2015 by Lawrence Raab. Reprinted with the permission of The Permissions Company, LLC, on behalf of Tupelo Press, tupelopress.org.

Lines from "Relics" are used by permission from *Somewhere Else* (Coffee House Press, 2005). Copyright © 2005 by Matthew Shenoda.

Li-Young Lee, excerpt from "Nativity" from *Book of My Nights*. Copyright © 2001 by Li-Young Lee. Reprinted with the permission of The Permissions Company, LLC on behalf of BOA Editions, Ltd., boaeditions.org.

Radmila Laziæ, excerpt from "Anthropomorphic Wardrobe," translated by Charles Simic, from A Wake for the Living. Copyright © 1998, 2000, 2001 by Radmila Laziæ. Translation copyright © 2003 by Charles Simic. Reprinted with the permission of The Permissions Company, LLC on behalf of Graywolf Press, Minneapolis, Minnesota, www.graywolfpress.org.

"Rhythm Method" from Pleasure Dome: New and Collected Poems © 2001 by Yusef Komunyakaa. Published by Wesleyan University Press and reprinted with permission.

Ruth Stone, excerpt from "This Strangeness in My Life" from In the Next Galaxy. Copyright © 2002 by Ruth Stone. Reprinted with the permission of The Permissions Company, LLC on behalf of Copper Canyon Press, www.coppercanyonpress.org

Trauma and Memory: Brain and Body in a Search for the Living Past by Peter A. Levine, published by North Atlantic Books, copyright © 2015 by Peter A. Levine. Reprinted by permission of North Atlantic Books.

When My Body Was A Clinched Fist

Enzo Silon Surin

Black Lawrence Press

CONTENTS

Acknowledgements..........xii
Birth of A Clinched Fist..........4

I

Elegy for One Sixty-First Street..........6
Corners..........8
Born to Triggers..........10
Letters to A Young Fist..........12
My Body as A Clinched Fist..........16
Stick-Up Kids..........26
Chotsani..........28

II

High School English 32
In A Fisted Universe..........33
Banking in Jars..........35
Legend of A Full Fist..........37
A Space Boy's Lament for Hoops Without Nets..........39
High's Cool English..........41
Pathology of A Clinched Fist..........42

III

Pathology of A Clinched Fist..........44
Passport to Brooklyn..........46

Elegy for Frankie..........48
Corners..........50
Damnified Field Theory..........51
Elegy for Frankie..........53
A Long-Awaited Answer to A Long and Painful Fight..........55

IV
Pathology of A Clinched Fist..........58
When Lead Became the New High..........59
When Lead Became the New High..........61
Glum Blocks 62
Letter to A Young Fist Contemplating Suicide..........63
How to Make a Fist a Microphone 65
How to Nullify A Super Hero..........67
Up Against the Wall, '94..........69

V
How A Fist Became A Spirit..........72
Elegy for A Clinched Fist..........74
Ballad of the Sad Young Fists 76
On Sunday Autumn Afternoons in Jamaica, Queens..........81
When the Body Returns as A One-Hundred-Year-Old Fist..........84

Notes 89
About the Author 90

ACKNOWLEDGEMENTS

My sincere thanks to the editors and staff of the following publications for first acknowledging the poems (some as different versions) in the manuscript:

The Breakbeat Poets: New American Poetry in the Age of Hip Hop: "Corners"; *Interviewing the Caribbean*: "Born to Triggers"; *Jalada/Transition Magazine, Issue 05/123*: "In A Fisted Universe"; *Jubilat*: "Birth of A Clinched Fist", "Legend of A Full Fist"; *Naugatuck River Review*: "On Sunday Autumn Afternoons in Jamaica, Queens"; *The Next Verse Poets Mixtape Volume One: the 4 x 4*: "How to Nullify A Super Hero"; *Pangyrus*: "Passport to Brooklyn"; *Soundings East*: "Letters to A Young Fist" (published as "Letters to A Young Thug"), "High's Cool English"; *Tidal Basin Review*: "High School English", "When Lead Became the New High" (published as "Death at a Fruit Stand on Market Street").

My deepest gratitude to the Boston Foundation and the Brother Thomas Fellowship for their generous support.

Much love and many thanks to the friends and mentors who inspired and influenced this manuscript and kept me from that permanent clench through encouragement and conversation: Shawn Narcisse, Orlando De La Mota, Chotsani Williams, Annette Reagans, Darlene Perry O'Neill, Tyesha Matthews, Bruce Low; Bonnie Hirschhorn, Janice Weinstein, Edward Butscher; Elijah McNeal, Edward Roberts, Lance Williams, Mary Marceau Wegmann.

Many thanks as well to the friends, poets, writers, and mentors who believed and made this collection possible through their encouragement and thoughtful feedback: My life affirming poetry connective, The Next Verse Poets (Melanie Henderson, Fred Joiner & Lisa Pegram); Shauna M. Morgan, Mary Hutchins Harris, Anastasia Guadron, Georgia Pearle; Afaa Michael Weaver, Danielle Legros Georges, JD Scrimgeour, with special appreciation for Cate Marvin for her gentle yet persistent insistence, without which the depth of most of these poems may not have been reached.

Finally, this is for my heart foundation, my family. You are the reason for my open hand.

for New York City
&
for Greg, Frankie

In the case of acute trauma, there are "hardwired *emergency responses* that call upon our basic survival instincts in the face of a threat. These fixed action patterns including bracing, contracting, retracting, fighting . . ."
—Peter A. Levine, PhD,
Trauma and Memory

Birth of A Clinched Fist

Born in epidemic—circa 1986 Jamaica,
Queens—when tiny white caps filled—
modern-day cotton—moored most under

a parking lot's dim cone of light—when
paraded in chambers of those born to triggers
was that sin which weaned father

from son; tricked out the best in us—
a resilient few kept from boxes,
though what was left was worsted in haze

on those horrid nights—when what was
promissory was plight was norm,
and what was dealt—mnemonic so strong

I kept it in my mind like one rehearsing
lines in an orograph for pain—
a pain, like bait, that turned gain

into the cleanest demise—when I stood
to cleave it, the fight empty as cavity,
the strife—marked by omission. Everything

I saw was enemy—even this face, fair game.

I

These changes explain why traumatized
individuals become hypervigilant to threat
at the expense of spontaneously engaging
in their day-to-day lives.
—Bessel Van Der Kolk, M.D.,
The Body Keeps the Score

It is another place and you are not
what you were but as though emerging
from the air, you slowly show yourself
as someone else.
—Ruth Stone,
"This Strangeness in My Life"

Thrown in the corner. Turned inside out.
What is indispensable and what is less so
Thrown on top of one another.
—Radmila Lazic,
"Anthropomorphic Wardrobe"

Elegy for One Sixty-First Street

Five furious years after Grandmaster Flash
penned a rap about edges, you zigzagged
the corners on runs for Benson and Hedges,

back when the zeitgeist of the block was crack
and your father had that used pale-blue Pontiac
he would dash the family into on Friday nights

trying to counter the myopic pull of the block's
high danger of dope fiends and the debilitating
euphoria in a whimsical gaze waylaid like mazes.

You sat in the back seat and uttered under
your breath *why would anyone ever trade in*
nights under palms trees for these qualm nights,

for the menacing overtone of a smile without teeth?
Because you've come to learn the most important
lesson is to master your own gaze, and strut, for

the days when soon enough you'd be spit back
onto the same strip of block where twice
a woman with eyes belonging to that dragged out

and quintessential gaze proffered you an act of
fellatio for five dollars. You were ten years old
on an errand to buy milk in a flagitious galaxy

but carried the weight of her bid on all future
quests to the grocery store, when the concrete
sparkled like a sky full of stars under your feet.

You were grateful for the drift of Friday nights,
when street telemetry took a back seat to the only
sign of life, a magnificent breeze against your face.

Corners

Outside Papi's Bodega, young boy in
summer's native garb—white tank-top,

doorag's a smooth blue crown garnishing
the stubbles of a week-old fade—regulates

a stereo knob while sitting shotgun
in a chromed-wheel Escalade—the ghost

of Tupac Shakur magnified in a sub-
woofer like an opus—as long as

music's kept *all's good where we come
from.* If only a glare didn't easily stumble—

if only manhood wasn't tenured with black
powder in metal capsules, brown boys, free

to chase arcade mortality, wouldn't have to
warily long for a ghetto's heaven or if grief,

inherited each day they step into the a.m.,
would follow them into an afterlife.

But corners often treble the soul, a cold hope
in the fold & on Winthrop and Thorndale

the sidewalk pleats, stumbles a man in hooded sweat-
shirt and blood-sodden jeans, fresh breaths

breaching his lungs—if only keeping eyes off
the karma and on the prize was what made this

world go 'round, it would be what was always
wanted—any landscape better than what's here

—where on most nights, a native glare renders
a chamber empty as winter flower boxes.

Born to Triggers

Long before the recoil,
at the sound of gunfire
the body tucked and ran

as if the volleyed pre-text
of trauma already vetted
your legs—not certain of

the way—away or toward
the mass—the riot within
the riot within—you ran

until *don't run, they'll shoot
you!* interrupted the assault—
hard asphalt 'gainst your feet.

You were nine and did not
know the body was capable
of such things on its own or

the catalog it would amass
in the nine subsequent years
when you'd surmise: some

days the body is a clinched fist,
at other times it is a doorknob
leading out and, there is no

such thing as a real shortcut
to the way back home—dis-
covering, when bullets or fists

come, one momentary hiding
after another—the first tuck
knuckling its way into the next.

Letters to A Young Fist

\#

Caution begins with summer's opening
—front stoop's clatter a family reunion:
slaw and fish fries—clacks of dominos
and c-low finger snappers on a deck—
little girls' double-dutched cackling
sidewalked—ice cream truck rocks its bells
attuned like a good friend's record making
its way down the street. And what is more:
week incites a Correctional release—fuse's
a vengeful chump—fallout, matter-of-course:
headlights eclipse—your sect called out—
from the barrow of a stoop, chrome's broadcast:

brace yourself—a whole new day un-caged
—your best friend no longer needs his name.

\#

The elegance of white tank-tops—gone
—a body's wailing authors calm to riot
as tymbals of Cicadas roar torrentially,
muffling last gasps—friend's last grasps,
a phantom reach. What the mouth devours
under a fallible street lamp—silence. His

absence will be the silence of resting soil.
A barrel-n-hammer rancor awaits you—
number of squeezes, unknown. How swift
the brass tacks' delivered to your brain
primes the next step—bands the parts of you
left—a gruff truth: love calls for counterblow.

Riddled with fought-living is thug-life. And re-
venge ≠ redress, nor is proof of anybody's love.

\#

It's what corners do—swelter—when
in custody of breath-takers—slugs, slugs...
Read the headlines verbatim—the names
at edge's front page are all names you know
by heart—you pushed weight with them—
c-notes brought all sorts of appeal—now
poised for retribution, your palms moist
as mouths—this story is narrated only
with caskets, fought-written—another truth:
this form of grief centers on topography—
anger's grief's impassable, an infinite wallow
—being asked of you? Make lead the new high.

Read the headlines for measure—remember
the streams poured; the premature exits.

\#

Before you sign your name on chalk
outlines, know this: the shape you
mold your hand to hold a gun is
the same as to sway a pen, to cup a yawn
or knot the lace of a doo rag—it's hard
to ward grief off—to know when—
harsh decisions commission loss—knotty
if you're not taught bona fide truths about
the world—how it owes you not one thing

—read this letter ad nauseam—corners
always do what they do best—the test's
rigid—what you practice becomes moral.

Before you sign your name on pavement
know that, this partnership, is permanent.

My Body as A Clinched Fist

I – Affliction

It was a gust—no a burst
of air—that brought the coil
to my hands time and again
and no matter what I did
to flex it didn't budge
and almost always brought me
back to Leon walking besides
me, then, in one svelte motion
not there, except for the treads
of his shoes making its way
down a street he didn't know
was a one way—the wrong
way—when he doubled back
it was clear that something
cannibalized the way home.

I vetted the treetops for a place
to perch, a vantage point beyond
the crowd that had gathered to
watch the fight but there was
no "fight"—it was all one-sided
~~seven ten eighteen~~ twenty pair
of fists and timberland boots
bared down into the boy and the
only sight of fight in him was his

body balling up like a fist to
brace the rush of even more
fists. What could I do? What
could I have done? They had begun
to also cannibalize passersby and
onlookers. I did what was customary:
collected faces for the diurnal course—
when there'd be another way to put fear
and the cheers into a vista that wouldn't
involve more fists. That day never came.
And when a fury this strong begins
to court a young fist, when anger's
calibrated with fondness for rancor,
there is only one end: to fight monsters
you must yourself become a monster.

II – Aftermath

There was no sign it ever took place
—no dents in the universe, no visible
wounds from where the paratroopers
landed their blows, no traces of Leon
no parallel bruise in your ribs, or spine,
—just beautiful, beautiful, beautiful sun

—no physical wreckage, shards of bone
no raging fire or smoldering carcass
just an echo in your bones and veins,
in the fists you packed for the day—
just sun, beautiful, beautiful, beautiful
sun—no shortcuts, same streets same

trees and you, staring at yourself like
the body's purpose was to harbor this
universe of cavity—wide enough to muse:
maybe there was still a way, so certain
there was still a way to walk away or
undo what was done—but with no body,

no witnesses no one to talk to no Leon
back at school—no sign the universe was
ever disturbed, except in your bones, and
in the loaded fist carried in your pocket—
you sat in class, reviewed homework like
you always did—later at recess, in that

odd beautiful, beautiful, beautiful sun,
whispering to the ball in your hands—
shot taker and rebounder—because even
at 13 you already knew that sometimes teeth
are a gateway to the city of one's own under-
standing and other times they are a gate

for what ails—and with no credible witness
to corroborate, other than your own reflections
in storefront windows—the ceaseless parading
of two bodies—a balancing double barrel pair
of fists—you settled into the glaring aftermath,
alone, glazed, in that beautiful, beautiful, sun.

III — Metamorphosis

When a burst of air is enough
to make your hand tremble
or when the wake in your jaw
is from sharpening one tooth
against another in your sleep—
to face a teeth-to-cheek world
that brings clots, hunger to jaw-
bone blocks—you realize no part
of the body is immune, not even
air in the lungs. The pressure and
heat accost because the fear and
sorrow of trying to walk away
that day had fused to your DNA

—first heat and first pressure came
with the first swing or first Timber-
lands or knock-offs—same width,
same assault—on the chest—when
Leon gasped you gasped and when
he flinched you flinched—the weight
alone of boots on his ribs should've
killed him but didn't—though some-
thing callused that day, conjoined—
and when the crowd broke away you
broke too—one version went home,
did his homework, and was good
the other still on the lawn trying to
be less like a young birch perched

and brazening through the boreal
climate and the body's consequent
retaliation. In one body, there's a boy
fleeting—in another you are that boy
ratifying, ratifying, ratifying the way
back home on that paltry afternoon,
in that erring, beautiful, beautiful sun,
when your body's genesis of an open-
and-close season exposed the hours
of expand-and-constrict, until all that
was left was the index finger, primed—
its new delegation as terminal member.

IV – Retaliation

When the body has had enough—
before the recoil into a ball of dust
or ash—when it is in full revolt—
some of the tucked impressions
one tries hard to contain emerge
as shakes or episodes of mania—
rushing back like blood suddenly
pooling in Leon's eyes two days
before being jumped, when a near
scrimmage in the hallway was
squelched, thought to have died—
but in one svelte motion the block
was rendered gridlocked.

Fists over a glare matured into markers
for measuring seasons and would later
be the reasons why you'd wake one day
a bit mean—didn't know yourself, and
had new hands, and had new feet—
finding yourself running down a street
in a rum frenzy—white moon haloed
against black, smoky sky—tangled up
in the waylaid traffic of recall: fists over
a glare—Frankie sabered into an infinite
goodbye—air pressure in full distress in
your lungs—dust filling gaps of motion.
When the body has had enough, mind

retaliates: under the glaze of a perpetual
and beautiful, beautiful sun, jejune fists
turned maulers bid Leon into a cosmic
gutter wide enough to muse that maybe
he made it out from under their blows
and maybe Leon is sitting somewhere,
blazed, growing bald on a head once full
of braids, musing on a roach and talking
shit about when he schooled them suckas
with a pivot and you are remembering
only what almost happened—not how
your entire body commenced a tucking
rotation until it became a full-fledged fist.

V — Revolution

Once a year I am reminded to
put flowers on the body's knuckle
grave—do this to remember being
young, fisted and afflicted, for years
spent taking the long way home to
avoid brandishing the self that made
walking these streets an endless bout
between the ghost of a childhood and
a new body of evidence. Nobody tells
you that no matter the outcome, every-
body dies in these streets—*it's a pithy
hand—the letdown's grime happens all
the time*: perfecting that b-boy stance,
hoping it would one day build a descrier
out of best guesses, all the years I walked
to school with haste as the myopic pull
of loiters accosted my legs into shortcuts
and retreats—glazed in that beautiful,
beautiful, beautiful sun: the body is a fist
is a fist is *a pithy hand in a drag-out bout* is
a fist is a fist is a fist is a body is a fist is a
fist is a fist and is never satisfied—so many,
too many fists: Greg, Leon, Shawn, Frankie,
Subrock, Foe, Angel, Jamal, Tony—write
their names to remember bruising *so easily
inside—it's a pithy hand, a drag-out grind*,
the body is a fist is a fist is a fist is a fist
the body is a fist is a fist is a fist is a fist

the body is a fist is a fist is a fist is hiding
from the heinous world...outside—*don't pry,
'cause in these hands a bid or tomb's brilliant
reprise*—the body is a fist is a fist is a fist
the body is a fist is a fist is a fist—and *they
are blind and they can't see* the body is a fist
is a fist is a fist—the body is a fist *it's a pity,
a dragged-out bout; it happens all the time.*

Stick-Up Kids

On a day when the heel of my Reebok
knock-offs flapped the film of a miserable
glue, three small faces—affixed to bodies
no taller than a doorknob, no older than
seven—faces belonging in brag-about-
my-children wallets—bore a panoply
of scowls to coerce pocket change.

Thought it was a joke—kept on walking,
dragging the one foot and crept the other
where my sock, visible through a hole
in the sole, collected shards of dirt on
Hillside and Parsons—until one pulled
a knife, threatened to ration out my chump
change, his four-foot frame against me—

his face a mask of street dust and salt-dry
sweat; other two hoarding as much fear
in their eyes as my pinky, which amassed
unawares into a fist. But I was eleven and
wanted nothing to do with laying it on the
amended versions of myself, in Petion-ville
three years before, hunger gulling cells

in my body. We stalemated. I kept watch—
up and down the street—one hand as bluff,
the other fending for space, for abeyance.

Some say they enjoyed the game too much.
These countless aims often lead to processions.
Did anyone consider these boys befitting claim,
not aim; worthy of belonging to a childhood?

Chotsani

Un-kissable, those girls found me,
puberty planting a minefield of pimples

in the greasy wasteland I called *face*.
I flattered myself in origamic smiles

lobbed across my desk, on their way
to other boys like pretty-boy Tony

or Angel and his alleged peach-fuzz.
I imagined love notes returning to me

at the same rate of Julio's 4-40 speed
or thugs like Jamal, who—when not

hustling quarters for lunch or spit-
polishing his fresh white New Balances

—had a habit of pulling out his penis at
school assemblies. They all got the girls.

I was always a friend—never a (wink)
friend or "friend"—never rumored to have

ditched class for the dank, dingy basement
where those very same girls made out with

boys who preferred flesh over words, who
took bets on whose panties they'd roost first.

But you were different and favored words,
sexy when you spoke geometry on walks

through the projects, your lips forming
decagons and parabolas—my ears sycophants

of vowels. Never more than boon companions,
you in Cross Colors, me in fake Adidas and

my brother's hand-me-downs—anomalous
in our abandonment of sadness, like the day

I ran home, with Frost in my lungs, to where
your voice, underscored by telephone,

emblazoned Mary J. Blige's *Love No Limit*.
Didn't you know you were a cosmic fantasy,

there behind those braces and that steady,
mindful gaze? Never thought I'd fall so evenly,

an unimaginable mooring, your backpack
on soft shoulders for moments when a nation

of words was what we needed to navigate
Junior High's dark and greasy wasteland.

II

There's always someone waiting
to bring back all the old fears—black fists
slamming like stones into black bodies
—Gary Jackson, "Cornell"

All the shouting before
was done out loud, on the street,
and now it's done so shushing-ly
—Ada Limón, "Down Here"

When the brain's alarm system is turned on,
it automatically triggers preprogrammed
physical escape plans . . . By the time we are fully
aware of our situation, our body may already be
on the move.
—Bessel Van Der Kolk, M.D.,
The Body Keeps the Score

High School English

After Charles Wright

Byron escorted from the pages,
ambulance siren falling away
                         through the frost window.
Peer at the clock, alter your route home—long poem.
What carries you, a lonely ascent
for which the objective's clear: regard both time and
reason.
The streets pole toward hue and cry,
                         the trek becomes infinite.
Better to mean what you say than to say what you mean.
Conceal your syntax, bid no explanations.

———————

Tomorrow's a standard deviation.
Where we live, the weight of which

depends on small silences
we fit ourselves into.

In A Fisted Universe

Would have thought we were trained
for the shots we took—fists tossed
into the blind bend of neck-n-shoulder
where truth held more misses than hits—
most of which was more show than blow.
Sometimes, as if on cue: a spot broke open
in the crowd amidst drawl and grimace—
and the withdrawn drew their card into
the dark matter of an ever after—triumph
or defeat, no one ever cried, as if the body
only attended to the tear and break and not
to tears. Most of these bouts, staged in empty
school lots—fists flaring their stellar remnants—
begat not one bona fide winner—fight within
as bitter as any in the ring. And the one
thing that always survived were lies told
about whose fists were hindmost—not
how easily hearts, under guard, went into
flip mode over a fresh pair of white sneakers,
and how some were eager to pledge homage to
a posse—didn't matter the cause or if one really
believed in the push of fists over bodies—one day
you'd be next. And some years from this moment,
the sound of something breaking or some poor boy's
plea will awaken lessons learned in science class,
about sound travel in space—myths of how
one can witness the destruction of the world

without hearing a single sound—how one can *wail*,
wail, *wail*, and no one'd be able to hear it. But you
know this to be claptrap—in space or back lot,
you can always hear the blare of your own ruin.

Banking in Jars

The first time I thought about
whittling down a high-five
into an eternally sealed conclave
of five finger bandits
was the day I found out why
my mom stopped going to banks—
the strong-arm at the ATM
to withdraw what was her last.

Rehearsed my vengeance in grips
made from that rancid air in the attic,
where I sat sweating and gauging
the amount of pressure to an imagined
temple or the stress of my knee bend
on the center of their back—penance
for fear and panic they placed in her,
the year she started banking in jars

around the house. Then there was
the brick waylaying in my bag when
canvassing the block, searching for
confessions on faces—before long,
trek had spread to a few more streets
and almost every face fitting the mold
was a head game. I balled up into a fist,
cooked up a makeshift smile and lied

about my whereabouts, for weeks, clinched
in the scuffle that births inside in moments
like these. But my mother knew that and
knew how to listen to the calm voice of God,
when night brings more than slumber to sons
who take their shifts on the edge of an elegy;
she knew—it's why she quietly banked her
tears around the house for an entire year.

Legend of A Full Fist

The memory of my first fight
is unreliable like a first kiss
or first fist full of marbles
in a Petion-ville courtyard.

Where other tales embellish
mine is feeblish—filled with
phantom swings and cheers
—no bruised knuckles or ego

to speak of. A first kiss begins
and ends with a lie about not
the falling in but the fallout—
it's not gracious or eloquent

when it flees—no matter the grip.
Even in the courtyard it flees:
a stock of marbles in a pair of
sweaty palms is not to be trusted.

Before the lag or knuckle down
there is no way of looking past
the look in another set of eyes
when they've got nothing to lose.

But you learn. Sometimes, you do
just about anything to avoid the fight

but not when it finds you in a pair
of gym shorts and Jeff is bumbling

something about your mother.
I swung but can't remember if
I landed any punches or if the pave-
ment simply clipped his clumsy feet.

So, I tell it like a tale about a first
kiss—with no trace of a bruised
ego or fright—or like the story
of routing a rival playing marbles

omitting the fact he was the nephew
of a *Tonton Macoute*. No matter
the courtyard, stories about full fists
are always more legendary than true.

A Space Boy's Lament for Hoops Without Nets

When you are taught
your body is celestial
and your rightful place
is among the demigods

you look for signs of life
in the most unusual places
sometimes redeeming a smile
when, barely, you can make

out a young boy's light as he
inbounds a ball back into play
and he nods back, not knowing
once you step onto the court, all

the fun will taper off and banter
will descend into cracked jokes
about you being high, shooting
air balls, which, with rims without

nets resemble made shots. A lament
will follow and hound his next set of
moves and there would be no glory
that day in his ill cross over or faded

jumper—winning's suddenly an elegy,
in waiting is a thoughtless wail to no
avail, the semitones of his pleading—
I wanna go home, I wanna go home,

I wanna go—and it wouldn't, didn't
take long before everybody needed
permission to be themselves, whether
they would admit it or not. It might

be a look or a slip of the tongue or hand
in the dark matter of the paint or black
hole of the three-point line, and they'd
be rendered silhouettes on a proctorial lot.

High's Cool English

We fit ourselves into
small silences, the width of which
depends on where we live.
Tomorrow's standard deviation:
bid no explanations, conceal your syntax.

———————

Better to say what you mean than to mean what you say
 'cause the trek here's infinite.
The hue and cry of the streets pole toward
regarding both time and reason—for which the objective's
   clear:
a lonely ascent—another long poem—alter your route,
conceive of a clock's whirr
       in a room of frost windows,
ambulance sirens falling away,
Byron escorting you back to the pages.

Pathology of A Clinched Fist

Total Recall

a fist is a palm's flight is thrifting through the chapters of a cold hurt is trying to bring into focus your obit is fright contained in the hue of an eye is a ruse for oozing a crocked mouth is for wielding class hoards like a mallet is kowtow of the street is rising from that is maybe another qualm's recourse is trying to get through an oblong block of uppercuts soaring near-at-hand to the incudes at the center of the ear is witnessing the destruction of the universe with both hands over one's mouth trying to conceal the blare of one's own ruin

III

Memory, when reduced to its most vital function, has to do with securing a future that chooses *selectively* from the past
>—Peter A. Levine, PhD.,
>*Trauma and Memory*

We are a memory shaped by vertebrae
Clappers of rhythm disassembled by the skeletons of time
>—Matthew Shenoda "Relics"

The days of our childhood together were steep steps into a collapsing mind.
It looked like we rescued ourselves, were rescued.
Then there are these days...
>—Claudia Rankine,
>*Citizen: An American Lyric*

Pathology of A Clinched Fist

Hypomnesia

who rode the blue streak
of the Q44 bus through
Flushing's coved meadows;

hopped the chain-link
to the narrow, graffitied
alleyway—to empty parks,

where dangled—without nets
—tortured rims dub as an altar
for malice; who stroke—a tireless

calm on Linden Boulevard's
canvas—that nod for consensus;
drew a clearing for larynx, and

a wide way leading out—called it
road; who airbrushed winter's brief
over-comb of a body's pallid streaks;

who blotted up the steam of sub-
way grates; righted the somber,
cab-less wave—grazed fingers
with guile, amber, *amber!* minded

the dab of calico corners in claret,
and traced the library of Jamaica's
gnome-filled streets—graved them,
upholstered a frame & called this home?

Passport to Brooklyn

Have you forgotten which bus takes you
down Flatbush Avenue—ballpark where
on Saturday afternoons, a beer-bellied
mechanic rounded the bases all the way
home—your no-hitter stashed in his pocket?

Have you forgotten buying knock-offs
and bootlegged mix-tapes on Jamaica Ave,
nights spent crushing cardboard in the back-
room of Payless with the Dread—late night
dollar-cab rides—beef patty, champagne

cola on your breath—the whims and warps
of New York City potholes? The flavor
of quarter-waters staled when you tried to
unlearn the same strut that made Danielle
wanna have your baby—it kept even real

thugs at bay. You have forgotten nights,
riding shotgun in Shawn's Peugeot—
daydreams of Rose's sister—two years
younger, a poet—who at fourteen, spell-
bound you to her doorstep, long after

lights would bail. Streets of whatever city—
names you no longer recognize—no matter
what corner you're on—when you can't

seem to find a good bodega or the way back,
find the vial of scented oil in your pocket

—flicking the cap's dull black enamel—
the one Frankie gifted the year Wu Tang
Clan's *Protect Ya Neck* bellowed from
his headphones in the back of English—
the year before he was stabbed to death.

Elegy for Frankie

When you first died—not
easily convinced—brokered
a deal—made a promise—new
egress—that didn't leave gashes
in muscles built in gym class.

Second time you died—still
needed convincing—knowing
it would be a matter of time
—before fists would canvas
the streets—black and blue.

Third time you died—almost
convinced I knew—who did
it—gathered mental footage
—acquaintances, relative to:
how they spoke, what was said

—some had their ways. Certain,
one day, reliably—in the locker
room—you stepped to that dude
with a baleful nod—was always
averse to banging—still paid.

When you died a fourth time—
down in the kitchen—clutched
a blade—tired of you in that alley—

kept it lightly against my stomach,
pressed harder—later, harder still.

Two decades ensued—toting enough
sadness for two—*just give me a word*
—you think it strange, this grief?
A maggot in the ear canal whispers
of severed arteries—pomegranate pulp.

You are still dying—grief an infinite
number of goodbyes—the qualm's pit:
what of the treble clamoring for ears;
what of my hands, inept in curbing
a newly found affinity for cold things?

Corners

On West Bryn Mawr and Broadway
someone calls your name, an ugly strut
commands his legs—your own imagines

water, buckles—sudden night crawler
behind a stretched row of parked cars.
You grow neck-first without a face

under the shield of broken street lamps,
heart's galumphing *thump thump thump.*
You hear your name again—rougher

—unlike a call from someone next door
or that of a friend freelancing a stopover;
gargoyle in you gargling. Will you breach

the quiet, boast your crew? If only there
was another way to make the nights glow.
How long will you lie there pretending

to swim? Steady your breath—minutes
from now, a sharp pop will render
another you hospital bound. Unfinished,

block to block a fire-back—sirens
declaring your whereabouts all evening.

Damnified Field Theory

Don't paint yourself into a corner
would imply one has a choice, a say
in the selection: the brush, paint, and
in the room—corners to edge one's
body's sharp elbows and knees into.

A choice is not a choice if one does
not have a say in the options—if we
did we would be gods. But no matter—
ardent vow or ache for calling one
another *God*—we were not. What

we were taught, it was wrong. I recall
playmates who made a corner their
epistle and grappled with knowledge
of survival not being in the strength
of an arm, or in the thickness of clothes

but in how often one succumbed to
the ruse of believing heaven was too
far up and out of reach, that one did
not deserve it. We were taught all
corners were bad places where idle

things collected dust. Yet New York
City was filled with many such rooms.
Could it be our demise was planned?

And choices we made not choices but
decisions, and selections made were

a consequence of not being ones to
father options? A room with such
corners isn't a city, isn't a choice
when all signs point to hell, just a
few blocks away, in every direction.

Elegy for Frankie

morning, mute—
*never ask
why*. In the grim

summer heat,
standing over
a mock trial of bones

—what my neighbor
dubbed a rat hoedown—
memoirs of an errant air

resumed in plumps
on a sodden canvas,
miles and years from

once-home. I stare long
and hard into burrows
where rats violate fence—

in three places—rehearsing
their death sentence as I did
with new york city when

the last savor of your lungs
was the alley air.

***

miles from trash day,
between thresholds
and flowers, rats

enter—my dogs give
chase—delve between
weed, mortar, majestic

chicken wire—resilient
little bastards on surrogate
ground for murder—

load the bait—every day
it's either me or them—
someone always has to go

—narrow trenches keep me
from pulling triggers—perhaps
law-of-the-street should've won

out—howbeit this time, I have no
intention of leaving this air accosted.

A Long-Awaited Answer to
A Long and Painful Fight

Some nights I find myself googling for obituaries
of friends estranged, missing or gone. Afraid
of what I might find, I am cautious with signs

of life: accomplishments, job promotions, Face-
book statuses—maybe a throw-back Thursday pic
would reveal they're still pushing breaths and not

what we feared those years back on Hillside Ave
in Queens, how easily a breeze on back of a fresh
Caesar resembled a girl's breath or a sneak attack.

In a world of *decepticons* and *nasty criminals*
same longing that brought us together kept us
vigilant, always an eye out for a switch in stance—

with one's back to the world, it meant someone
had to watch it. Too many dubbed *Last Seen*—
the fight within as deadly as ones in the street.

When I click on a photo with a familiar name,
speculating body mass index & age progression,
I am relieved to find the over-weight white real

estate broker from Florida or the middle-aged

elementary school teacher from Pennsylvania
with the out-of-time headshot. It means some

may still be suspended in the vortex of moist
breaths in a pair of hands, back when rumors
of our early demise doled out a turbulent truth.

IV

Salutation and farewell
in a single glance.
    —Wisława Szymborska, "Travel Elegy"

out of what little earth and duration
out of what immense good-bye,
each must make a safe place of his heart
    —Li-Young Lee, "Nativity"

such things not only shatter
and rebuild people's minds
but also their bodies—simply, it would appear,
because the body is also a system of habits.
    —Edward Carpenter,
    The Art of Creation

Pathology of A Clinched Fist

Anamnesis

a fist is a pound is for pounding is a knock is a pocket of moist breaths in winter is a peephole is a cupped cough is a delegation of five allies is a flag for black power is for talking under one's breath when the conversation turns sour is a city of five boroughs is a grip is a jab is a boxer is a champion is a weapon is an impostor is a body-of-blows sponsor is a tuck season is a hide-n-seek playpen is a pen of five little piggies is a strike is a palm balled up is a hand balling uncontrollably with its trigger finger tucked in its own mouth.

When Lead Became the New High

It was clear, when the choice of jabs
was no longer how the streets wanted
to propagate its math, and any plausible
retribution for Leon and Frankie meant
a shift into an implausible plot.

Posses had lost their lure—too many
beefs to track, too many hurt feelings,
too many dull claps and nights when
slap boxing bled into a lush trap of fists.

Then days of fists deliberately strayed and
latterly gave way to triggers: a gat meant
bolstered ranks, divorcing the cut-throat from
the posers; gats meant few waylaid for kicks—
the pint-size and meager now capable of pushbacks.

Before that one could scrap but now a gat
meant you could be your own posse—win
or lose, the block was soon on that *somebody
gotta die* tip. And it was apparent the blitz
gave rise to some real gangsters, who engraved
best-by dates by setting their clocks to breach:
a crossover at the park or a prolonged gaze
could bring more than bruises to one's ribs.

It was clear the trek was no longer about
who was next to fall—or rise—but when.

When Lead Became the New High

A confectionary yellow haze had offered up
the afternoon wholesale when a sage-green
sedan with tinted windows rims around the corner,
driver fresh with lead in his lap—who two days before
rattled AG's rear bumper, after which, a rumpus ensued,

and suddenly AG, a straight-A student, was sent to stay
with his grandmother for the summer, who on that day
was out for a bag of fruit, which now dances an esoteric
dance across the pavement, as two bullets ventilate AG's

chest—block rendered a three-ton gridlock—
the when of which began with a crackling
commotion, over a clunker of a *whip*—
eighty-six Mazda to be exact, with a smoke-and
-tear muffler—double parked near a fruit stand.

The story not fully told is that the heart
is a purpling bass drum filled with liquid,
and grief, a daily rough draft, as plums
in a cotton net bag wither in a drain.

Glum Blocks

after Aimee Nezhukumatathil

Something had stirred up the self
brought up to respect the hand's reach—

urban tagged into a friend's blue meditation.
He watched your back all the way

into a violent karma—*no time to make a way*,
to blink. Learned none but one way

to rebate a face, not once to snooze a hand
on hollow blocks where muzzles flashed—

in one svelte motion, *your boy is gone*;
a bummed glock bound to his *saynomore* plea.

By winter, the cold vetted you
a bummed glock to walk the stiff grass—

healing has gone and numbed—the way
to not want to kill is tethered

with tape. It's hard to curb this mean
when a simple turn of head makes

all the difference. All those eyes.

Letter to A Young Fist Contemplating Suicide

when there is nowhere else to go but back
into the corners of the body's sanctuary city

when every time you turn around it's your back
up against the wall, it's days spent in tuck and

rotation—forgetting the seasons of being open
enough to touch—when you know too well how

it feels to wake up with an apocalypse inside
& the Eros of being gully—how the struggle

often breaks into a factory of tears without
warning—when it takes just a word or gaze

to make a joke out of the promise someone
will always love and care for you, when you

learn quickly the limitation of hymns, a fear
bigger and wider than your eyes and mouth,

when the sound of your heart beating sounds
like footsteps on good days, and on bad ones

like boots stomping on some poor boy's chest,

when you start to remember how many eyes

were watching, how many hours are left in
days filled with beautiful sun and collapse,

know that you are the last light before dusk,
know that the body is an essay of bones to be

read alive—best when read alive—and you are
not supposed to die your natural death like that.

How to Make A Fist
A Microphone

after Nina Corwin

A bass-less rant's as good as a chipped tooth
to get haters off your back. Bottom-line, winner takes all

with a little bit of coercion—once the beat has accosted
you must bring those suckers to their knees.

When the DJ drops the needle end get a whiff and heed
to the mob's qualm like nobody's business.

What we have here is more than a bioclimatic rupture—
a whole sordid lot of rhyme schemes, bopping heads 'til
 they're gaslit.

Spitting with the most poise moves the crowd *holla if you
hear me.* Next dis is gunning for the neck.

If the call back's weak, pass the mic, claim an exit,
'cause not all rhymes are make-believe or punch lines
 legendary—

know a leering may await your set; battle won but no re-
spite—a bruising attitude can open a way, *treble treble*,
 boon flips.

And suddenly it's you against the world—tragic camisado browbeating the lungs in a skirmish, all to protect your rep.

How to Nullify A Super Hero

At the edge of a bed's stoop—
pillowcase cape, plunger
as dagger—avenger of wrongs
interrogating a whimsical city

filled with sirens and choppers,
cops dwelling in dark alleys—
stymied in ambush of ski-masked
robbers. Imagined your superhero

telephone ringing, a frantic voice—
Shawn, who lived down the hall,
—in need of help to bolster late-
night raids—dreamt of being a cop,

the raiment of NYPD blue—wanting
to bring solace to a uniformed hue
Haitian families akin to the *Tonton
Macoutes*. That would change.

Calling out to phantom crooks—
lay down your weapons—your best
Lion-O from the ThunderCats voice—
awing at a sky urged into clamor

with your plunger—playing the part
'til the wind that framed your chocolate

milk-mustached face tucked you
into bed—a decade long slumber.

*

When you woke up, Shawn no longer
wanted to be a cop and your dagger
breaking news: Abner Louima—
arrested outside a Brooklyn nightclub—

hand-held radio and fist-battered—
later at a precinct, plunger's handle
—sodomy. Later still, interrogation:
his brown body sluggish as yours,

eyes swollen in that eclipsed room.
Started fearing that you had entered
the wrong skin at birth—into a
blunt country, a barrow world—

musing on Batman and Robin—what
did they do on their off days, when
out of frame, with their utility belts,
in Gotham's whisted and dark alleys?

Up Against the Wall, '94

Years gone by and—*don't give
them a reason*, is all that you can
say—still words don't come easy

when the interrogation lasts longer
than the actual minute it should take
for hands to make their way around

and down your chest, when the weight
of both penis and pistol pushed against
your back distracts you from the other

pair of hands between your thighs and
hot breaths so close you feel moisture
dewing on your cheek and can make

out both what they had for lunch and
the tang of aged urine and sweat on
the wall, when you can't see but feel

eyes clocking your arraignment and
the city behind you feels like a gone
world and your weeping becomes

a dreary lake in a valley of pimples—
when you know looking like someone
who fits the description is another way

of saying *they can do this* and there is
nothing you can do about it, & when
an engram of an apology fails to greet

you after, not the first nor second time,
nor the third, you know the person who
fits the description will always be you.

V

You travel beyond to childhood,
measuring accomplishments
but finding only images
to be mustered and arranged
—Kwame Dawes,
"House Arrest"

Grateful to be standing there, letting
the moment pass through me
as if that was all that had to happen.
—Lawrence Raab,
"Last Restoration"

does it not seem clear what a power a new
feeling or thought may have and may exercise
in disturbing or readjusting the organisation of
the body?
—Edward Carpenter,
The Art of Creation

How A Fist Became A Spirit

Somebody must have finally told
God what these boys were up to
on one hundred and sixty fourth
street, after all the years they made
a living dodging the bum-rush

of payback on streets they collared
and tethered, calling themselves
the A-Team for their precision in
carrying out beatdowns, known for
what they hid in pockets, for sucker-

punching some passersby into a coma
without fear of karma or reverence of a
higher power, brandishing swagger for
all to see the devil was alive—we knew
& felt him scheming, desperately trying

to pry the caliber of praise from our mouths.
We were young and didn't know any other
story's end that didn't involve piggybacking
off paybacks and learned to read footsteps
on pavements and the currency of long looks

and the omen of fist prints without notice
even if our allegiance went way back
there was also a way to turn friends into

distant strangers. So, when Greg fumbled
his arms from a b-boy stance to greet me

there was no way of knowing, a boy who
who was unafraid and mastered the chorus
of fists over a glare, would one day learn
a new song—though it was clear he had
not learned how to pry that old tune from

his eyes, it was clear when he spoke that
he had thoughts about tomorrow, though
his body boasted the yesterday of the blocks
we grew up on, with posses, baring dubs like
Decepticons, Down to Kill, & *Nasty Criminals*

and names we swore we'd boast for life like
foe, subrock and *black capone;* put them on
walls and store gates, as reminders of who we
were, for days when words were hard to come
by and we'd forget the meaning of *forgiveness*,

how to ask for it—*don't turn out like me,* he said.
There was no way of knowing that his words would
eventually build a descrier out of the years I walked
to school and back with haste, as the myopic pool
of loiters accosted my legs into shortcuts and retreats.

Elegy for A Clinched Fist

Every June we bid farewell to a class
of fists whose return was not promised
—some due to grade graduation and others
to the myopic pull of fisticuffs, as if the year
was academic tuition for the bigger bout to
come. When one punched in—crown scuffed
& bereft of jewels, like a wounded beast pining
for respite or an aged champ without his gloves
or ring, without his usual prowess or fanfare to
canonize him—it was clear that an indivisible
sorrow or wound kept him tucked, pocketed.

Other times a last look, was, and the only
future was one plagued with rumors about
a bid (if lucky), change of venue or at times
an ultimate blow that could foul up even a
grown man's soul—at thirteen or fourteen
this was thought to be more hype than threat,
but many names were not called at graduation
or out at roll calls in September. Some mused
aloud as refuge, others mouthed a silent elegy,
just in case rumors were more water weight
than bone—because they knew these kings,
whose habits of launching swashbuckler bids
into crowds, whose fists still haunt the trail
of the way back, since there's no such thing
as a whilom king, just dead or exiled kings

or forlorn kings without kingdoms—and any
mention of their names or deeds, was enough
to wake the one within, the one that knows too
well fist against face was how they kept time;
and is one reason why you have never attended
any class reunions, opting instead for the ruse
of coursing through yearbooks, to eulogize and
to dust the wrangling grave of your adolescence.

Ballad of The Sad Young Fists

for Greg
after Pablo Neruda

1.

Some days, like a birthday—days that carry
the difficult light that we haven't died—
won't let us forget
nights we kept up at all hours
with claptrap and tales
and no regrets.

Those days are better when we've forgotten
hands that decimated with the force of a clap
or litany of blows, when sun betrayed trust
and one couldn't help but spike the quarter-waters
drank as proof we were still offspring—
days when a skirmish bequeathed its knack
for boasting glories so clear so bold
a sideways glance felt like the world
'bout to claim its revenge.

There was love in the midst, it moored us:
the lean, the banter, the vastness and eccentric
bliss of thuds, the mute biotic ether
ushering in that reticent gone gone.
Some days we were the gone, akin to goodbyes

that harassed us, compelled some and crowned few.
We woke into new folds every morning.
We wake still amassed in ghostly wrinkles.

    2.

Vernacular that erode us: thugs, marauders...
We navigated through provincial terrors
and through the gauntlets of the too-soon-
gone—body's token-and-breath vernacular
a disdainful woe in each departure,
like a welder's torque, the blistering seal.
In truth, most trekked along the barrel convinced
a better place was in the chase.

And some days, the rays would pry
open hands until the sun felt like
a glimpse of salvation—same hands
that without their reign/fought-living could
have claimed fewer effigies and withstood
the love of an un-claimable turf, and
also the back streets that married most
to a bout's toll often settled on knees.

3.

The inertia termed and vernacularized
us, obituaries still clung—dirges sung a capella.

We saw to it to eat up the short-lived
grime on the occasion the perpetual
grind changed its course and we had to brave
a millimeter's posited rain with no umbrella—
some got bold at the threat of graves,
some reprieved the hurt, courting a retreat
that belied fear, some bereft of their heartbeat—
It was a bruising lull, this haul, this pushing ahead
akin to ruse, this defeat—its lag
and its tow.
Fact that we survived—
to grow fat
to grow old
after rounds
of bicker led to the ascent of a fist milieu
onus on the body—confounds us. Then there were
the rumors: cuffs on the wrist riddled dreadful clots,
being knocked unconscious into a singular, hapless
and feeble return, helpless and in
a frightful place among other sad young fists,
who bled on jail floors in valiant effigy.

4.

Also, in effigy, annals of grin
on those harrowing nights
we became brothers, navigating these roads
where blows for looks were like candy, part trap-
culture—the haze that kept us lax yet punchy
cocky and Novocain-ed.
The streets alone offered us:
a pound-for-pound brand of love
for what tangoed inside us,
and dealt those not willing
to perdure, an ephemeral joy.

5.

What was said of our lives
became creed: *calculative deviants?*
Like the weight in our hands was
something we dreamt up?
Like the haze always led to brags?
In truth, in the folds of a rolled-up sleeve
was the hope we'd out live
the hard rain, the constant shine
of a world filled with malice—
being aware how we all could disappear
in the underlying aims
of the block's seasonal curve

where every day felt like autumn had arrived
and we were the leaves.

6.

forgive us for wanting to
share the glory of midlife
extending hands in walkabouts—
same hands
that kept time in blows,
brought floods—
did you know:
each drop
in the flood
was thought to be a way?

or that none of us expected
to have made the cut?

On Sunday Autumn Afternoons in Jamaica, Queens

we trusted
our bodies cutting into
the fat bold air

in hand-me-down
layers—pigskin
against our ribs

like a Hughes' weighted dream—
no pads, no helmets for the journey
of grabs and leaps. We toiled

until the field faded—and
alone and out of breath,
we talked and laughed, waded—

the accumulation of out-and-gone days
—some of the things we'd never said
said, as if this would carry into real life.

The whole self was a current, a fragile cargo...
and I was there, waving, and I would be there at
the other end

—Naomi Shihab Nye,
"The Whole Self"

When the Body Returns as
A One-Hundred-Year-Old Fist

Somewhere in the broad counting of seasons
spent as a clinched fist, I open to my oldest son
looking at a one-hundred-year-old poplar in the yard.
He says "daddy, the tree's pointing at me." I say
to him "that is one hundred years pointing at you",

after which he uncovers and holds up a discarded
branch, counts the number of buds & says "this is
twenty-five years old." Not sure how he arrived at
that number—a minute before he asked if we would
all die by end of summer, four months from now.

He is only four years old. These days, everything
seems divisible by four: Before our two sons, we
had two dogs—Cassius and Louie—four days ago,
Louie died four weeks after Cassius passed away,
so we're back to being four again, and so my son's

thoughts are on streaks of losses. I was his age when
I experienced my first loss—when my dad left Haiti
to build what he hoped would be better life in New
York City; mom followed a year later, and it would
be another four years before my brother, sister, and I

joined them. Then there were four of us—youngest
sister, born in the States, four years after my dad left
Haiti—this was nineteen-eighty-six, year of the Miracle
Mets & the Chernobyl disaster. Four years later Leon
caught a beat down after school from the boys on 164th

street and my body began its first tucking rotation—
it was nineteen-ninety, the year that two different songs
titled "Hold On" went number one and "Wind Beneath
My Wings" won a Grammy. In another four years Frankie
would be stabbed to death. These events always seemed

to coincide with the year of the Winter Olympics—like
clockwork always divisible by four. Twelve years later,
the year my mother died, I contemplated suicide and
salvation in the back pew of a church, the year I also
met my wife—and four years later, dad had a stroke

almost four months before the wedding—don't remember
much except my father dancing all night at the reception.
Two years later, a terrible bike accident interrupted
the count—wasn't my time—filled with thanks for
miracles—we had a son the following year—fortunes

turned—the relentless numbering of growth ensued.
Four years later, we had our second son, who is four
months old as I write this. Somewhere in the broad
counting, one wishes life was more poetry than prose.
I'm down to four working digits on both hands and

winter makes it painful to write, or hold, or point, so
I am grateful for four seasons. But it is again the year
of the Winter Olympics and I wish I was making this
up: I have entered my fourth decade of life; my second
born son is four months & my first born is four years

so, when he tells me the tree from which the twenty-
five-year-old branch came from is pointing at him,
I asked the only thing one could ask when a hundred-
year-old tree, which, like my body, has survived many
clenched fist seasons, seemingly returning to the same

shape, & greeting the various, abhorrent winters, in full
preparation of an omen that is always divisible by four,
and with an inner clout that may not take another bout,
& with clear expectation of this tree informing our new
definition of optimism—I asked, "did you point back?"

NOTES

1. "A Long-Awaited Answer to A Long and Painful Fight" is titled after a line from the song "Fallen" by Sarah McLachlan.

2. "Ballad of The Sad Young Fists" is titled after the song "The Ballad of The Sad Young Men" and is modeled after Pablo Neruda's poem "Still Another Day" as translated by William O'Daly.

3. "High School English" contains the lines "*depends on small silences / we fit ourselves into*" from the poem "Rhythm Method" by Yusef Komunyakaa.

4. "How to Make A Fist A Microphone" is modeled after the poem "What To Pack For The Apocalypse" by Nina Corwin.

5. "My Body As A Clinched Fist" contains lines inspired by the adlib lyrics of the late and great Nina Simone, as performed in one of her renditions of "I Wish I Knew How It Feels to be Free".

6. "Passport to Brooklyn" contains the refrain "*you have forgotten*" inspired by the poem "When You Have Forgotten Sunday: The Love Story" by the late and beloved Gwendolyn Brooks.

ENZO SILON SURIN, Haitian-born poet, educator, publisher and social advocate is the author of two chapbooks, *A Letter of Resignation: An American Libretto* (2017) and *Higher Ground* (2006). He is a PEN New England Celebrated New Voice in Poetry, the recipient of a BrotherThomas Fellowship from The Boston Foundation and a Denis Diderot [A-i-R] Grant as an Artist-in-Residence at Chateau d'Orquevaux in Orquevaux, France. Surin's work gives voice to experiences that take place in what he calls "broken spaces" and his poems have been featured in numerous publications and exhibits. He holds an MFA in Creative Writing from Lesley University and teaches creative writing and literature at Bunker Hill Community College. He is Founding Editor and Publisher at Central Square Press.

www.ingramcontent.com/pod-product-compliance
Lightning Source LLC
Chambersburg PA
CBHW021955090426
42811CB00001B/31